FIRST THINGS REPRINT SERIES
Christianity Face to Face with Islam
by Robert Louis Wilken

Copyright © 2010 by First Things

This essay is adapted from Professor Wilken's 2008 Erasmus Lecture, sponsored by First Things, and was originally published in the January 2009 issue of First Things (35 East 21st Street, Sixth Floor, New York, New York 10010).

First Things' web address is www.firstthings.com.

About the author:

Robert Louis Wilken *is the William R. Kenan Jr. Professor of the History of Christianity at the University of Virginia and a frequent* First Things *contributor.*

Christianity Face to Face with Islam

Christianity Face to Face with Islam

No event during the first millennium was more unexpected, more calamitous, and more consequential for Christianity than the rise of Islam. Few irruptions in history have transformed societies so completely and irrevocably as did the conquest and expansion of the Arabs in the seventh century. And none came with greater swiftness. Within a decade three major cities in the Byzantine Christian Empire—Damascus in 635, Jerusalem in 638, and Alexandria in 641—fell to the invaders.

When reports began to circulate that something unusual was happening in the Arabian Peninsula, the Byzantines were preoccupied with the Sassanians in Persia who had sacked Jerusalem in 614 and made off with the relic of the True Cross. And in the West they were menaced by the Avars, a Mongolian people who had moved into the Balkans and were threatening Constantinople. Rumors about the emergence of a powerful leader among the Arabs in the distant Hijaz seemed no cause for alarm.

Even on the eve of the conquest of Jerusalem, when Arab armies had encircled the holy city and blocked the road to Bethlehem, the patriarch of Jerusalem, Sophronius, assured the faithful: "We will laugh at the demise of our enemies the Saracens [as Christians first called the Muslims] and in a short time see their destruction and complete ruin." Fourteen hundred years later the Muslims are still in Jerusalem, and with each passing decade Islam figures larger in the minds of Christians, penetrates more deeply into Christian societies, and, by its fixed and impermeable tenancy of a large part of the globe, circumscribes the practice of Christianity.

From the day Caliph Umar was met by the patriarch Sophronius in Jerusalem in the mid-seventh century, Christianity has found itself face to face with Islam. Though the circumstances have varied from place to place and century to century, Islam has always presented a challenge. Yet, in the course of a long history, during which Islam expanded all over the world, Christians, with the exception of those who lived in the Middle East in the early centuries of Muslim rule, have seldom taken Islam with the seriousness it deserves or recognized it for what it is—a religion in the biblical tradition in which piety is wedded to statecraft. A "complacent ignorance" (in the phrase of the modern scholar Lamin Sanneh) has prevailed, especially in the West.

Before the Muslim conquest, Christians could look back confidently on six hundred years of steady growth and expansion. By the year 300, churches were found in all the cities of the Roman Empire, from Spain and North Africa in the west to Egypt and Syria in the east, as well as in Asia Minor and the Balkans. In the fourth century the Armenians embraced the new religion, and on the eastern shore of the Black Sea the preaching of St. Nino led to the conversion of the Iberian royal house and the adoption of the Christian faith by the Georgians. To the south, Christianity reached Ethiopia in the fourth century and Nubia a century later. And there were Christian communities in Roman Gaul already in the second century and in Britain by the third century.

No less impressive was the spread of Christianity eastward. Accustomed to the colorful maps of Paul's missionary journeys printed in study Bibles, we are inclined to think that the initial expansion took place in the Mediterranean world. But in the vast region east of Jerusalem—Syria, Jordan, and Iraq, where Aramaic was the *lingua franca*—the majority of people had become Christian by the seventh century. The Christian gospel was carried even farther east to ancient Persia, and from there it traveled along the Silk Road into Central Asia: Uzbekistan, Tajikistan, Afghanistan. At some point during the first six centuries it reached the western shore of India and even China. In the seventh century, the global center of Christianity lay not in Europe but to the east of Jerusalem.

Though the peoples of this vast area spoke many languages and had different customs, through Christianity they were linked together in the confession of the creed of Nicaea. They baptized their infants in the name of the Father and of the Son and of the Holy Spirit, offered the sacrifice of the Eucharist in their churches, were governed by bishops, revered the lives of ascetic men and women living in monastic communities, and had in common a holy book.

Archaeologists have uncovered fragments of ancient Christian texts that make the point powerfully. At both Antrim in Northern Ireland and in Panjikent, near Samarkand, in present-day Uzbekistan, copybooks were found from about the year 700 (wax on wood in Ireland and potsherds in Asia), each containing verses from the Psalms. In Ireland, the schoolboy whose language was Irish had written the psalm verses in

Latin, and in Panjikent, the boy whose language was Soghdian had written his lesson in Syriac.

When one considers the extent of Christianity in the year 600, the deep roots Christians had set down all over the world as they knew it, and the interconnectedness of the churches, it is no wonder that Christians had difficulty grasping that the Arab armies occupying their cities were not simply conquerors seeking booty but heralds of a spiritually potent religion and architects of a new civilization.

The first recorded comment of a Christian reaction to Muhammad dates from only a couple of years after his death. When tales of a prophet among the Arabs reached Christian Syria, someone asked an old man, "What can you tell me about the prophet who has appeared with the Saracens?" The old man groaned deeply and said, "He is false, for the prophets do not come armed with a sword." He had in mind of course the Hebrew prophets, Elijah or Isaiah or Amos. A prophet is one called to *speak* for God.

But his memory of the Bible was imperfect, for he had overlooked the greatest of the prophets before Jesus: Moses. Like the later prophets, Moses was certainly called to speak for God, but, unlike Isaiah or Ezekiel, Moses was also a political and military leader and, let it not be forgotten, a lawgiver. And he carried a sword: In the Book of Numbers, we learn that he armed a thousand men from each tribe of Israel to take vengeance on the Midianites.

It is this biblical prophet, Moses, who was the model for Muhammad. Though Muslims see Abraham as the first to believe in the one God—and thus the first *muslim* and the ancestor of the Arabs through Ishmael—the prophet mentioned most often in the Qur'an is Moses. Muhammad was, like Moses in the words of St. Stephen in the Acts of the Apostles, "powerful in words and deeds."

And the early spread of Islam was an affair of deeds: vigorous, venturesome, irresistible deeds. In the span of less than a hundred years, Arab commanders made their way from the edge of Egypt along the North African littoral until they reached the Atlantic Ocean. From the Arabian Peninsula they also advanced northeast through Persia and across the Asian steppes to India. The Arabs reached Sind, today a province in Pakistan, in 711. And within the same decade, after crossing the Straight of Gibraltar into Christian Spain, they crossed the Pyrenees and penetrated southern France, to be halted finally at the battle of Poitiers in 732.

By the beginning of the eighth century, Muslims had created in these disparate and distant regions a new community formed by common beliefs and practices and held together in a loose unity by the caliphate established in the ancient Christian city of Damascus. As new territories were conquered, garrison towns arose. The Arabs brought their wives and children, built mosques, and over time founded such new cities as Basra and Kufah in Iraq, Fustat (old Cairo) in Egypt, and Kairouan in Tunisia. By keeping themselves apart initially from the local societies, they were able to maintain their identity in a sea of strange people and gradually displace the culture that had dominated the region for a thousand years.

Soon Islam began to take hold among the conquered peoples—and one reason was that they were already familiar with the biblical tradition on which the Qur'an drew. For example, an entire surah is devoted to the biblical Joseph, the son of the patriarch Jacob, viceroy of Egypt.

At first Arabic was spoken only by the Arabs, but by the end of the seventh century, during the caliphates of Abd-al-Malik and his son Hisham, Arabic became the language of administration, commerce, and learning as well as of religion. To replace the Byzantine currency, gold coins were minted with Arabic legends carrying a reproach to Christians: "There is no god but God alone. He has no companion." A public cult supported by political authority was established, calling for an annual month of fasting, prayer five times a day, recitation of the Qur'an on Fridays, and the *khutba*, an address before prayers.

In other ways Abd-al-Malik claimed the public space for Islam. In a dramatic political gesture, he built the Dome of the Rock on the Temple Mount in Jerusalem, altering forever the skyline and character of the holy city. On interior as well as exterior walls, inscriptions emphatically proclaim the central tenets of Islam. "There is no god but God and Muhammad is his prophet." The phrase "God has no companion," an explicit critique of the Christian doctrine of the Trinity, occurs no less than five times. Abd-al-Malik also appointed judges to administer the emerging body of law on matters of ritual, marriage, inheritance, and property. Over time, the law of Shari'a, more an evolving body of social practices than a fixed code, became a defining mark of Muslim identity. Its significance for the Muslim is as much psychological as legal, which helps explain why it packs such emotional force in Muslim countries to this day.

Within the space of a century, the movement inaugurated by the prophet Muhammad had planted a permanent political and religious rival to Christianity in historic Christian lands. Its advance both to the West and to the East meant that a large part of the globe was claimed for Islam, fulfilling the words of the Qur'an: "We appointed you successors on the earth after them." For Christians these territories proved irrecoverable. Four hundred years later, when the Crusaders arrived in the East, the Arab historian Ibn Athir said that they had entered "the lands of Islam."

Little of this was apparent to Christian observers in the early years, or at least few were willing to acknowledge what was happening before their eyes. John of Damascus, who lived during the reign of Abd-al Malik at the beginning of the eighth century, wrote a polemical account of Muhammad based on his reading of the Qur'an. But in his book he places Muhammad in the section on "heresies" and depicts him as a descendant of the arch-heretic Arius: a teacher of a truncated version of Christian truth. At some abstract level that may be true, and it does show that he thought Islam and Christianity share a common spiritual lineage, but it is noteworthy that he treats Muhammad solely in theological or religious terms, ignoring the cultural and political changes that he wrought.

About the same time, a monk writing in Syriac in the region of Basra had a keener sense of what Islam meant for Christians. In a dialogue between a Christian monk and a Muslim official, he has the Muslim official say: If your religion is true, "why has God handed you over into our hands?"

By the year 750, a hundred years after the conquest of Jerusalem, at least 50 percent of the world's Christians found themselves under Muslim hegemony. In some regions, most notably North Africa, Christianity went into precipitous decline. At the time of the Arab conquest there were more than three hundred bishops in the area, but by the tenth century Pope Benedict VII could not find three bishops to consecrate a new bishop. Today there is no indigenous Christianity in the region, no communities of Christians whose history can be traced to antiquity. Though originally conquered by the sword, most of the subject peoples eventually embraced the religion of their conquerors. By a gradual process of soft coercion, Islam was able to gain the loyalty and kindle the affections of those who were subjugated and make them part of the Muslim *umma*—no small accomplishment.

In greater Syria—including the Holy Land, Egypt, and Iraq—the rights and privileges of

Christians were limited by their legal status as *dhimmis*: members of a restricted and inferior minority subject to an onerous tax. Still, Christian intellectual life flourished. In the early centuries under Islam, Christians participated in the vigorous and enterprising culture being created by the Muslims. They gradually made the transition to Arabic—a delicate undertaking, because much of the religious vocabulary in Arabic came from the Qur'an. They wrote apologetic works in defense of Christianity and engaged in debate with Muslim thinkers on points of practice, doctrine, and philosophy. Even a partial listing of Christian thinkers writing in Arabic during this period is impressive: theologians such as Theodore Abu-Qurrah (a bishop in Harran, in southeastern Turkey) and Timothy I (catholicos of the Church of the East in Baghdad), such translators as Anthony David of Baghdad and Stephen of Ramlah in Palestine, and such philosophers as Hunayn ibn Ishaq and Yahya ibn Adi in Baghdad. Though their names have been mostly forgotten, their writings have endured, offering a precious resource for Christians as they address Islam today.

By the eleventh century, however, Christianity had begun a long demographic decline in its eastern homeland, and, carried by the militancy of the Turks, Islam resumed its relentless drive westward. The end of the eleventh century also marked the beginning of the First Crusade.

In recent years, there has been much moralistic posturing over the brutality of the Crusaders and thoughtless pontificating about their historical import. Out of ignorance, many conveniently ignore that the Crusades were part of a Christian counteroffensive against the occupation of lands that had been Christian for centuries before the arrival of Islam. In the Iberian Peninsula, Christians had begun to reconquer lost territories in the center of the country (including Toledo), the Byzantines had launched new offensives in Syria and Anatolia, and, further east, the Georgians and Armenians had rebelled against Muslim overlords. The Crusades do not stand alone; they were an understandable attempt on the part of the Christian world to halt the advance of Islam and reclaim Christian territory, including the holy city of Jerusalem.

But the Crusades ended in failure. For a brief period Christian kingdoms were established in the Holy Land and in parts of Syria, but in less than two centuries the territories were reclaimed for Islam. No doubt that is why Muslim memory (until recently) viewed the Crusades as a transient epoch, a regretful intervention by outsiders but less significant than the devastation brought by the Mongols. The Franks were simply another enemy. Only as the Crusades have been put at the service of contemporary agendas, both in the West and in the Muslim world, have they become viewed as a *cause célèbre.*

In the long view of history, and especially from a Christian perspective, the Turkish conquest of Asia Minor was of far greater significance. The arrival of the Turks prepared the way for the displacement of the Greek-speaking Christians in Byzantine Anatolia, the planting of Islam in the Balkans, and the fall of Constantinople in 1453. Though many books have been written about Constantinople, most notably Stephen Runciman's gripping narrative, little has been said about the gradual dissolution of Christianity in Asia Minor in the centuries leading up to the fall of Constantinople. There is no more heart-rending chapter in Christian history than this and, in the telling of the Christian past, none more completely forgotten—a reminder, as W.H. Auden once wrote, that "dreadful martyrdom must run its course in a corner." In poignant contrast to the Crusades, what happened in Asia Minor had far greater consequences, not merely as an event for historians and pundits to debate but in the hard intractable facts of demography.

Consider some statistics. In the eleventh century, the population of Asia Minor was almost wholly Christian. By the sixteenth century, Muslims constituted 92 percent of the population. During those centuries, the Church lost most of its property, its ecclesiastical structures were dismantled, and its bishops prohibited from caring for their dioceses. At the beginning of the period, there were four hundred bishops; by the end, 97 percent had been eliminated. Because there was no centralized state, only petty rulers, a *dhimmi* system was never put fully into place. As Muslim institutions flourished, the Christian population fled, and the disoriented and dispirited who remained gradually adopted the religion of their masters. Today there are only tiny remnants of ancient Christian communities in Turkey.

As a result of Turkish victories, by the beginning of the sixteenth century Islam had a new powerful political center in Constantinople and was putting down roots in southeastern Europe, where it remains to this day. The establishment of Turkish kingdoms in Asia Minor and the Balkans accomplished for the lands northeast of the Mediterranean what the Arabs had done in the countries on its southern shore, in greater Syria, and in the Fertile Crescent.

When Edward Gibbon introduced the prophet Muhammad in his *Decline and Fall of the Roman Empire*, he observed that the rise of Islam was "one of the most memorable revolutions, which have impressed a new and lasting character on the nations of the globe." Gibbon saw that Islam did not just inaugurate a religious revolution. Its unparalleled expansion changed the course of history by altering the map of the world and creating a new geography.

It is that singular and adamantine fact that we must ponder in thinking about Christianity as it faces Islam. A few years ago *National Geographic* published a handsome volume with the title *The Geography of Religion*. As one would expect, besides its beautiful pictures of religious buildings and of rituals from all parts of the globe, it also includes a map of the world. On it the continents are colored to identify the dominant religions in the various regions. India, for example, where 75 percent of the population is Hindu, is colored orange. Orthodox Russia and Eastern Europe are colored purple, and Catholic Latin America is colored lilac. But the largest contiguous area, colored green, is occupied by Islam, which occupies a huge land mass extending from the Atlantic Ocean in the West to Pakistan and Bangladesh in the East.

We are all familiar with textbook accounts of Christianity as a tale of growth and expansion as it spread from the countries on the shores of the Mediterranean into northern Europe, flowered in the high Middle Ages, was rent by the Reformation, crossed the Atlantic Ocean, was chastened by the Enlightenment, and then, in the wake of the great missionary movements of the nineteenth and twentieth centuries, underwent a period of phenomenal growth in the Southern Hemisphere and in Asia. In this rendering of the last two millennia, Christianity and the West sit atop the summit of civilization.

If, however, one injects into this sanguine narrative the story of Islam, things take on a different coloring. Set against the history of Islam, the career of Christianity is marked as much by decline and extinction as it is by growth and triumph. By a selective choice of periods, events, and geographical regions, the conventional account (the one imagined from the perspective of Europe and North America) gives the impression of continuous progress.

But seen in global perspective, that may be illusory. To state the obvious: Most of the territories that were Christian in the year 700 are now Muslim. Nothing similar has happened to Islam. Christianity seems like a rain shower that soaks the earth and then moves on, whereas Islam appears more like a great lake that constantly overflows its banks to inundate new territory. When Islam arrives, it comes to stay—unless displaced by force, as it was in Spain. But the shameful expulsion of Muslims from Spain is hardly an event Christians would wish to celebrate today.

There are exceptions, of course: Ancient Christian lands such as Greece, Armenia, and Ethiopia remain Christian. Yet when the matter is viewed geographically, these countries seem perched on the edge of a much larger and expanding Islamic world. There is good reason to be troubled over the supine acquiescence of Europeans today at the collapse of Christianity as a social and cultural force and over the mounting number of Muslims living in France, Germany, and Britain. Though Christianity was able to create a great civilization, it seems incapable of preventing its dissolution.

Europe's place in Christian history is singular and without parallel. Rome, the most hallowed city in Western Christianity, was the home of a Christian community at the beginning, as St. Paul's letter to the Church in Rome attests.

Centuries later, in alliance with Rome, Christians north of the Alps created Europe and, in modern times, European Christians and their descendants carried the faith to all parts of the world. And in the younger churches, at least in the early years, it was European forms of Christianity that were set in place.

Christianity has had an abiding physical presence in Europe. The bonds of affection are attached to place: Its churches, shrines, tombs, and pilgrimage sites were imprinted deeply on the Christian soul. The demise of Christianity in Europe and the ascendancy of Islam would be a crippling blow to the continuity of Christian memory and the sense that the Church is the carrier of an ancient, unbroken, living tradition that reaches back through time to the apostles and to Jesus. Memory is an integral part of Christian faith, but unattached to things it is infinitely malleable, even evanescent, like a story whose veracity is diluted as its particulars are forgotten. Without tangible links to the past mediated through communities tethered to the earth, something precious is lost. "Walk about Zion," sang the psalmist, "go round about her, number her towers, consider well her ramparts, go through her citadels, that you may tell the next generation that this is God, our God for ever and ever."

If Christianity continues to decline in Europe and becomes a minority religion, its history will appear fragmentary and episodic and its claim to universality further diminished by the shifting patterns of geography. And without the bridge of Western Europe, the Slavic Christians in Eastern Europe and Russia, bearers of the ancient Byzantine tradition, would be isolated from the Christian world. At the end of *After Virtue*, Alasdair MacIntyre wrote that we are waiting for another St. Benedict. In my wanton and admittedly darker ruminations, I sometimes wonder whether what Christianity needs is a not so much a new Benedict as a new Charlemagne.

But, of course, that is an idle thought. No matter how great the accomplishments of Christian kings and emperors, that chapter in Christian history is closed. True, one can point to the astonishing growth of Christianity in the Southern Hemisphere, especially in Africa and Asia, and to the unbounded enthusiasm evangelicals and Pentecostals have brought to the Christian mission. But energy and enthusiasm are no substitute for deep roots, vital and durable institutions, and a thick and vibrant culture. Will the younger churches have the staying power to pass on the faith in its fullness generation after generation and give rise to distinctly Christian societies? And how will they fare in the face of aggressive Muslim communities alongside which some live?

Which brings me back to the geography of religion. The Islamic revolution is more far-reaching than could be sensed when Gibbon was writing in eighteenth-century Europe. Take Africa, for example: Though Christianity came to Mediterranean Africa in the second century, with the exception of Ethiopia and Nubia it did not spread south into the continent. Islam, however, penetrated early into sub-Saharan Africa from Libya and Morocco and crossed the Red Sea from the Arabian Peninsula to Zanzibar to reach trading centers along the eastern coast of Africa. With its deeper roots, Islam has had far greater cultural influence on that continent than has Christianity. Here, too, looking at a map is instructive. Islam is dominant not only in North Africa but also across a band of contiguous states in sub-Saharan Africa: from Senegal in the west to the Sudan in the east and down the coast. When we hear statistics of the growth of Christianity in Africa, it must be remembered that they apply only to the southern third of the continent.

In Nigeria, for example, there are many Christians and the number is growing, but Christianity is a relative newcomer to the region. Where Islam traces its history in western Africa to the eleventh century, and a Muslim kingdom was established in what is now Nigeria in the fifteenth century, the Christian mission in Nigeria began in earnest only in the nineteenth century. The northern regions of the country are largely Muslim and share a common culture with the belt of Islamic states stretching across Central Africa. In recent decades, the Muslim population in the north of the country has grown increasingly assertive, calling for a wider application of Islamic law within society. This effort has been resisted by Christians, but in 1999 and 2000 various forms of Islamic law were implemented in twelve of Nigeria's thirty-six states. Muslims have also pressed Nigeria to join the OIC, the Organization of the Islamic Conference, an association of fifty-six Islamic states promoting Muslim solidarity in economic, social, and political affairs.

Of even greater significance is the growth and establishment of Islam in southeast Asia, in the archipelago between the Bay of Bengal and the China Sea. From India, Islam spread along trade routes into the region and, by the sixteenth century, Muslims had become the dominant religion in what is today Malaysia and Indonesia. Here Islam made its way not by military conquest but peaceably, through the gradual conversion of people who had contact with Muslim traders and through the quiet labors of itinerant Sufi preachers. With Muslim growth came Muslim culture and law and, eventually, Muslim rule.

In a way that is not true of Christianity, Islam is territorial. One of Islam's most enduring innovations was that religious law became also the law of the body politic. Shari'a is more encompassing than the Church's canon law, and historically its authority depended on a community with territorial boundaries and political jurisdiction. This understanding is of course being tested today and has been debated by Muslim thinkers since the nineteenth century. But most Muslims in the world live in countries in which Islam occupies a conspicuous public space in society. Even in countries such as India, where Muslims do not make up the majority, the feeling of solidarity and belonging runs deep.

There is a moment in E.M. Forster's *Passage to India* in which the British headmaster Cyril Fielding and his young Muslim friend Dr. Aziz are having a conversation about their different approaches to life. Fielding says, "I travel light." Aziz thinks: "So this is why Mr. Fielding and others were so fearless! They had nothing to lose. But he [Aziz] himself was rooted in society and Islam. He belonged to a tradition which bound him, and he had brought children into the world, the society of the future. Though he lived so vaguely in this flimsy bungalow, nevertheless he was placed, placed."

This sense of placement, of being defined by one's social world, is still very much alive among many Muslims. For centuries Islam has been the bearer of a spiritual and prophetic vision of the ordering of human society on the basis of worship of the one God. This vision continues to discipline the lives and marshal the energies of millions of people in different social, political, ethnic, and linguistic settings.

There is no sign that it is faltering today. As a religion, Islam has had remarkable tenacity. Although in science, in the humanities, in technology, and in statecraft the West has far outdistanced the Muslim world, the practice of Islam has not been dislodged by the political and cultural hegemony of the West. As Muslims have struggled to come to terms with modernity as we know it in the West, Islam as a religion has not gone into remission. The remarkable truth is that the peoples and societies that were part of the Muslim world five centuries ago have remained resolutely and unreservedly Islamic.

Turkey is a good example of the resilience of Islam in modern times. Here is a historically Muslim country whose constitution, law, institutions, schools, and mores were forcibly stripped of religion early in the twentieth century—reshaped to conform to a coercive secularism based on ideas of *laïcité* derived from the French. Religious teachers were divested of authority and religious schools closed. Men were required to give up the traditional head covering and adopt Western brimmed hats that made it impossible to prostrate in prayer. Women were forbidden to wear the veil. The traditional day of prayer and rest, Friday, was abandoned and Sunday put in its place.

In the last several decades, however, the practice of Islam has undergone a revival, and religious Turks have gained political power through democratic means. Though the roots of the Justice and Development Party, the present government, are Islamist, its leaders have behaved as centrists, and some have compared them to the center-right Christian democratic parties in Western Europe. Even the *New York Times* and the *Washington Post* portray their opponents, the secularists, as old-fashioned, ideological, and undemocratic. Almost a century after Kemalism, an authoritarian secularism, was imposed on the Turkish people, the overwhelming majority of the population remains Muslim, and Islam has reasserted itself in the public square. It is hard to imagine something similar happening to Christianity in Britain or France.

By focusing on what went wrong, on Islamic terrorism, on Wahhabism, or on radical Islamists, we miss ways in which Islam is adapting constructively to a changing world. The Columbia historian Richard Bulliet argues that, until there is a fundamental reconsideration of Islam, the word will continue to sound to Western ears "like a rattlesnake's rattle." If we see Islam as a historical relic, incapable of change and betterment, inimical to reason and science, a form of religion that is disadvantaged in the modern world, we will never grasp the formidable challenge it presents to Christianity. Bulliet calls attention to what he calls "edge" situations, areas of Muslim life where significant developments are taking place: in Muslim diaspora communities in Europe and North America; in democratically oriented political parties in Muslim majority countries, such as Turkey; and in education, either traditional religious schools or universities, as in Indonesia.

I am no apologist for Islam. Over its long history, Islam has been very bad for Christianity. In North Africa and Asia Minor, the arrival of Muslim armies led in a short period of time to the destruction of Christian communities. In the Middle East, *dhimmitude* was a suffocating institution that eventually sucked the oxygen out of communities, turning them in on themselves as they bent their energies to the sole end of survival. Although during the early centuries of Muslim rule there was fruitful intellectual and cultural intercourse, it did not last and has largely been forgotten. To this day a great part of the world remains effectively closed off to Christians.

Violence has been a persistent strain in Muslim history. Even as sympathetic an interpreter as Marshall Hodgson, in his magisterial *The Venture of Islam*, acknowledged that the vision of the prophet Muhammad "led inevitably to the sword." It is a "peculiar test of Islam," he says, as to "how Muslims can meet the question of war." So there is much to ponder and, for Christians living in the Muslim world, much to fear.

Given the experience of centuries, it is tempting for Christians to see Islam as the enemy. Often it has been the enemy. But if that remains our dominant paradigm for looking at the religion, we deny something of ourselves. Christianity's historic mission was to bring the worship of the one God, the God of Abraham and Isaac and Jacob, to the nations. Let us not forget that the first and greatest sin is idolatry, to worship something other than the one God as god. "You shall have no other gods before me," reads the first commandment. Christians confess, "We believe in one God, the Father, the Almighty, Maker of heaven and earth," and Muslims recite, "There is no god but God and Muhammad is his messenger."

The kinship between Christianity and Islam is deeper than the centuries of conflict would lead one to think. To mention only one example: the collaboration of Christians and Muslims in the ninth and tenth centuries in the translation and interpretation of philosophical works from Greek antiquity into Arabic and their transmission to the West in translations from Arabic into Latin in the eleventh and twelfth centuries.

The significance here is twofold. First, long before the major writings of Aristotle were known in the West, Muslim thinkers had appropriated the Greek philosophical tradition. The continuity of Western philosophical thought depends in part on the contribution of

Muslim thinkers. Second, because Islam, like Christianity, is grounded in the revelation of a transcendent God, a free creator, Muslim thinkers addressed a series of philosophical and theological topics—God and the world, creation out of nothing, the freedom of God, faith and reason—that Christian thinkers would also take up. The resulting dialogue raised the level of sophistication of Western thought and helped Christian thinkers clarify and deepen their own approach to similar issues.

Although the divide between Christianity and Islam is great and the search for a usable past looks unpromising, Christians must learn, as the bishops at Vatican II put it, to look on Muslims "with respect." For "they worship the one God living and subsistent, merciful and almighty, creator of heaven and earth, who has spoken to humanity and to whose decrees, even the hidden ones, they seek to submit themselves whole-heartedly, just as Abraham, to whom the Islamic faith readily relates itself, submitted to God."

Within the last two years, there have been two serious efforts by Muslim leaders to reach out to the Christian world. The first was an open letter to Benedict XVI a month after his lecture at the University of Regensburg. The violence that erupted in the Muslim world after the speech made the headlines, but the letter, largely ignored in the American press, was more significant. In it Muslim leaders from all over the world prepared an irenic, thoughtful, and critical response to the pope's comments on the use of reason—the heart of the pope's speech—and criticized Muslim extremists.

A year later, in fall 2007, a longer statement of Muslim leaders was addressed to Christian leaders East and West, Roman Catholic, Orthodox, Protestant, and Evangelical, entitled "A Common Word Between Us and You." In the long history of Muslim-Christian relations, it is unprecedented that a group of Muslim thinkers from different parts of the world and differing views should collaborate on a positive overture to Christians. From the beginning Islam has been a harsh critic of the central teachings of Christianity. "A Common Word Between Us and You," however, draws extensively on the New Testament to argue that Christians, like Muslims, teach that love of the one God is the first and greatest religious truth.

The authors link the words of the Prophet's message directly to the biblical tradition. In proclaiming "there is no god but God," these Muslim leaders write, the Prophet Muhammad was echoing the first and greatest commandment to love God with all one's heart and soul, as found in the Bible. "That is to say . . . the prophet Muhammad was perhaps, through inspiration, restating and alluding to the Bible's first commandment."

Still, Islam is more than a faith, and Christianity cannot relate to it simply as one religion to another without reference to social, cultural, and political factors. As useful as theological dialogue may be, one cannot ignore the facts on the ground. And the most significant fact is this: The vast geographical extent of the Muslim world offers an exceptionally sturdy base of piety, learning, and culture for expansion. It is often said that the great story of the twenty-first century will be the conflict between Christianity and Islam. From the partial view of these first few years in the century, that certainly seems true. But if the Islam we imagine is the one that makes the morning headlines or the evening news, our sight will be as constricted as that of the Christian inhabitants of Byzantine Syria when the Muslims began to construct a new civilization in their midst. Only if we move to a higher elevation to view Islam on a large historical and geographical panorama will we have the vision to take the measure of the determination, strength, and resources Muslims are likely to display in the decades to come.

Christianity cannot escape Islam's political geography. A part of the world will remain off limits for Christian witness, and the future is bleak for Christians living in Muslim countries. In the Middle East (with the exception of such countries as Egypt and Lebanon, where Christians are still numerous), Christians will have difficulty existing even as minorities. And in countries on the edge of the Muslim world, such as Nigeria, where Christians make up a large and growing part of the population, they will find themselves on the defensive as Muslims seek to implement Muslim law in society. And, of course, as their numbers mount in Europe, Muslims will be increasingly assertive in claiming public space for the practice of Islam.

The question to be asked, then, is whether, face to face with Islam, Christians will be able to sustain, rebuild, and create strong and resilient communities that provide institutional anchorage for the faith to endure and flourish. Will they have the imagination to form the spiritual architecture of the societies of which they are a part? This is a task for which Christianity is particularly well suited. It has a much longer lineage than Islam, it has taken many different cultural forms in the course of its history, and it has passed through the fires of modernity. It has a deeper and more coherent relation to its own tradition, including the cultural patrimony of classical antiquity. And it commands the intellectual resources to understand and engage other religious traditions as well as to provide moral inspiration for secular societies.

Unlike Islam, Christianity began as a community distinct from the body politic, and for three hundred years it existed independently of political authority. This early history has never been forgotten. Even in the time of Christian hegemony in the West, during the age of Charlemagne, Abbot Wala of Corbie insisted that the Church constituted a parallel sovereignty. The king, he said, should have public properties for the maintenance of his army, and the Church should have "church properties, almost like a second public domain."

Augustine's metaphor for the new life in Christ was not that of an individual's being born again but that of becoming part of a city with its own form of governance. "Happy the people whose God is the Lord," wrote the psalmist. Though some may eschew the term, in the decades to come the great challenge for Christians will be to fashion, within the cultural and political conditions of the twenty-first century, a new kind of Christendom.

More Praise for First Things

"The most thoughtfully reflective journal addressing complex issues of faith and culture."

—Timothy Tennent, President, Asbury Theological Seminary

"First Things continues to carry forward the distinctive vision for engaging and transforming the public square initiated by Father Richard John Neuhaus."

—David S. Dockery, President, Union University

"First Things brings freshness and light to the staleness and darkness of our contemporary cultural. Some of the most intelligent and articulate Christian and Jewish voices can be heard on the most pressing social and cultural issues of our time."

—Lyle W. Dorsett, Billy Graham Professor of Evangelism, Beeson Divinity School

"First Things is simply the best journal of its kind— rich in its intelligence, faith, and verve."

—Cornelius Plantinga, President, Calvin Theological Seminary

"First Things is exactly that. One of the first things I pick up to get in tune with what is happening culturally and religiously in our world. It deals with First Things first."

—Darrell Bock, Research Professor of New Testament Studies, Dallas Theological Seminary

BRAINSTORM!

.com

The discussions are engaging. The writing is lively. Visit **FirstThings.com** and kick-start your mind each day with the most stimulating content on the Internet.

FirstThings.com covers the crossroads where religion and culture meet. You will delight in reading the best thinkers and writers of our time engaging the most important questions of our time.

If you believe that ideas matter, if you want to be part of a conversation that is exhilarating, profound, and intellectually enriching, join us today!

FIRST THINGS
RELIGION, CULTURE, AND PUBLIC LIFE

Made in the USA
San Bernardino, CA
14 July 2016